LOVE SONGS OF CARBON

Born in Cornwall, son of an Estonian wartime refugee, **Philip Gross** has lived in Plymouth, Bristol and South Wales, where he was Professor of Creative Writing at Glamorgan University (USW). He has published twenty-six collections of poetry, eleven with Bloodaxe, including *Between the Islands* (2020), *A Bright Acoustic* (2017); *Love Songs of Carbon* (2015), winner of the Roland Mathias Poetry Award and a Poetry Book Society Recommendation; *Deep Field* (2011), a Poetry Book Society Recommendation; *The Water Table* (2009), winner of the T.S. Eliot Prize; and *Changes of Address: Poems 1980-1998* (2001), his selection from earlier books including *The Ice Factory, Cat's Whisker, The Son of the Duke of Nowhere, I.D.* and *The Wasting Game.* Since *The Air Mines of Mistila* (with Sylvia Kantaris, Bloodaxe Books, 1988), he has been a keen collaborator, most recently with artist Valerie Coffin Price on *A Fold in the River* (2015) and with poet Lesley Saunders on *A Part of the Main* (2018). *I Spy Pinhole Eye* (2009), with photographer Simon Denison, won the Wales Book of the Year Award 2010. He won a Cholmondeley Award in 2017.

His poetry for children includes *Manifold Manor, The All-Nite Café* (winner of the Signal Award 1994), *Scratch City* and *Off Road To Everywhere* (winner of the CLPE Award 2011) and the poetry-science collection *Dark Sky Park* (2018).

PHILIP GROSS

Love Songs of Carbon

BLOODAXE BOOKS

Supported using public funding by
**ARTS COUNCIL
ENGLAND**

Cover design: Neil Astley & Pamela Robertson-Pearce.

Digital reprint of the 2015 Bloodaxe Books edition.

for Zélie
from beginning to end

ACKNOWLEDGEMENTS

Acknowledgements are due to the editors of the following publications in which some of these poems first appeared: *Friends Quarterly, London Magazine, Magma, Manhattan Review, New Welsh Review, Planet, Ploughshares, Poetry and Audience, Poetry London, Poetry Review, Poetry Wales, Rabbit Poetry Journal, Raceme, The Arts of Peace*, ed. Adrian Blamires & Peter Robinson (Two Rivers Press, 2014), *The Bastille, The Book of Love and Loss*, ed. June Hall & R.V. Bailey (Belgrave Press, 2014), *The Compass, The Friend, The Poet's Quest for God*, ed. Fr Oliver Brennan, Todd Swift & Dominic Bury (Eyewear Publishing, 2015), and *The Wolf*.

With thanks to Janet Passehl for her work in ironed cloth, *Sleep* (2011), which was the starting point for *Thirteen Ways to Fold the Darkness*, and appears on the cover of this book. Also to Carole Burns and Paul Edwards for their project Imagistic in which this took place.

CONTENTS

Paul Klee: the late style

1

Came to painting on burlap, not for lack of fine paper or canvas.

See the effort of scraping the paint across that surface. Almost pain.

And the stuttering, crude and approximate edge.

His own skin drying: scleroderma. Paint on that.

2

The opposite of watercolour,
where juice and gravity take us

with ideas of their own.

But sackcloth... Paint that dries
before it's left the palette.

That has to be dragged, already crusted.

There could be despair in this. Or
freedom, knowing that already

we're too late.

3

The kettle drummer

he made almost nothing
but his drum.

Like the broadcasts hammering
the airwaves, nightly,
into the shape of a war.

Like waking in the darkness,

your heart thumping, but no
other edge to your body,
lost sensation of its borders

– just this, dull percussions
surging. In, out, sure as the tide.

If a tide could be dry.

4

If you can't help but hear the drumming,

if there's nowhere (even with the Alps
between you) at a far enough remove

then (as your canvases are hung

skewed – *decadent!* – fenced round
– *degenerate!* – with crude graffiti,

as your own skin tightens

on the bonecage) be
the bold bald mark on what

you can lay hands on, be

the drum skin
beating till it rips

5

still beating (don't say *beaten*) even then.

This body,

                    brute
fact, given thing

that winces sometimes
from the mere jolt of itself (joints thickening,
stiff gristle, nerve-ends bared)

against itself... This one,
the scorch in the veins

from inside like the moment
before fire takes, an agitating smoulder in the tinder,
out into the tightest far capillaries.

See it sensing itself
remote and close,

as an infrared scanner might spy
through roofs, to find... do I mean *me*? in hiding
or through earthquake-jumbled walls

as the rescue teams call, listen,
call. See our two (do we even

own them?) bodies sense each other,
waking in the dark; each would know if the other was gone.
We give out presence,

weather, transpiration. Life
is work and work

is heat, the one
sheer gift; we hold it here between us, just to spend
on, subcontractors to the sun.

Thirty Feet Under

Statistically, in the long view, we're in deep water,
  walking the brink of the lowest spring-tide low –

on seabed blinking, caught out, the sky in its face
  and parching it for... how few minutes in a year?

Not mud, but a curiously scrubbed crisp mudstone
  with fine tooled holes, slim bivalves well bored in,

snugly billeted. A desert mainly: no weed but a fringe
  of Dead Man's Fingers, blunt as cactus. Shells

like un-done washing up. Look closer: every other one,
  turned up, turns out to be a repossession,

the hermit crab squatting withdrawn in a bubbly funk
  with its cutting gear stacked at the door. Here,

there and there, holding its breath, a garnet gobbet
  of anemone. And us? We're a long way from home;

the cliff, the pier even, have a way-back and other-
  world look like an opposite shore. Statistically,

on average, we'd be fathoms under – odds against us,
  in the long view. And yet here we are: you, me. We *are*.

Mould Music

1

Alongside, always,

the air
invisibly alive

with them, these ever-
presences: mould spores...
They mean us no harm;

they have nothing to say

or sing but *Simplify*.
Or, in our terms, *Decay*;

lay down your intricate
molecules: fruit, meat.
skin flakes. Reclamation crew,

night-cleaners, makers-

and-breakers of what
we let slip... First the self-

engorgement of the peach
then its shrivelling.
In the moist, the dark room,

the ghostly blue-grey

of the lustre on the plum skin
is developing its imprint

of the after-life. Then again:
from a further remove
what's the shimmery bloom

on the rind, the lichen

on the rock in orbit,
but us: cave-

moss bristling
its tiny luminescence
in the black of space?

    2

Green-grey age-spots on the Perspex
                station awning
        make a sub-sky
under which we wait.

Each speck of bird muck starts its own slick
                where rain takes it.
        Small crude galaxies,
a curdled Milky Way.

Mould colonies as fertile and contingent
as the flood-banks of the Nile.

A year or two since this was new,
                clean, see-through;
        now, accommodating
to the state of nature,

almost as close almost as inside
                our own skins,
        as out of reach,
its interior weather

casts an aquarium light.
In it, no one looks well.

3

Exposed, developed. Variation. Re-
capitulation. In all
things, the silent sonata. Or
simpler:

a five-finger exercise, the great performer
breaks us down
to arpeggios: barcodes, black, white,
yes or no,

of the chromosome code,
its racks of fractal
demi-semi-quavers, not so much
the art of fugue

as the state of one; suddenly,
among its tireless tiny repetitions
a slip... And we're gone.
It's a matter

for us who *are* matter,
who hang
on each least note of it,
of life and death.

4

If we could just see it so: light
        sheeting up from the shipyard
behind high walls, the night
                shift flickering in arc flash,
        clash and clangour, the high
                ferment of it, where a fifty-
        year-old ship comes home to die;
the yard too is dying but picture it, more
        ritual than economics: the hulk
dismembered till they can't be sure,
                the old men, when to cease to call
        the ship they made by name.

Prime scrap for smelting, like our-
selves, if we could see. No shame
in the breaking, if we could stand far
or near enough, till who's to know
if that's the welder's spot, a crumpling star,
cell, or fused synapse, you, me. No
loss, if... if we *could* see it so.

5

Leave your still-life bowl of fruit

a little longer. Life, still. The nectarine
hints, one last time, at puberty.

Alongside, the end of last week's
white-sliced, its interior architecture,
its echoey corridors of substance,

is being broken, being broken down.
Like dewfall, this comes from the air,
any air, that lung-sip you've just taken;
impartial in its care, no fear or favour,

it *prevents us everywhere*. Yeasts,
moulds, our secret sharers, in our creases,
under finger and toe nails, most at home

in our moistures. In bread rising, leaven,
that came to our table from the cold,

the damp, the dark: the uninvited guest.

A Love Song of Carbon

For six years, on a high shelf in an upstairs bedroom,
    she was the only one who did not change.

Down here, in the oxygen economy, we came and went,
    our carbon still mixed with water, breathing, moistening,
        drying – yes, even our youngest, there, etching in breath

on the glass, now a smiley or down-in-the-mouth-now
    moon-face dripping. *He* took time, the eldest, withering

without her, needing ointments for his thinned
    and flaking skin – the sores on his shin did the weeping,
        the chemical bonds coming loose, letting parts of him go...

As patient as she'd learned to be in life, she
    waited, dressed and contained – in leather-textured

cardboard round a screw-top urn. Six years till the day
    they could meet in all simplicity, at last, entirely
        conversant with each other. Ash into ash

lifts from my broadcast scatter, and into a wet wind
    for winnowing, chalkier flakes dropping free

into wire-rooted ling, small gorse, bell heather,
    rabbit scuts; the finer grains fetched up (we
        flinch, then stay, yes, why not let them dust us)

lifting towards Sheepstor, North Hessary Tor,
    Great Mis Tor and the deeper moor beyond

whatever skyline he and she had ever reached.
    The rain clouds come up over Cornwall like the grey
        Atlantic. Generations. Wave on wave on wave.

for JKG and MJAG, 10.06.12

I Remember I Remember

...that there's a mist-horizon to it, there and not there,

the grey-brown hunch of Roughtor prowling
just beyond the redcurrant bushes, distant some days,

some days close up as if we were on its mind

...that *some* days was a great invention still to come,
like *remember* itself, that fundamental widget

with which, in time, I would operate the future

... that time was nearby like an old glum
babysitter, not unkind, but she never said much

except *Wait*

(the grandfather clock, meanwhile, had nothing
to say – like uncle Fred's fobwatch,

it imported nothing but importance, there

to be buffed and tinkered with)
                                        ... that days
precipitated, out of grey moist Cornish air

...that each hung from the dark top lip of window,

sometimes glittering, more often grey
with an upside-down world in it, tiny and shivering,

ready (in the space between the drip and no

drop yet) to fall
                        ...that when tick came to tock
the hills would slope off from the end of the garden,

to hide in geography
                    ...that memory itself

would be born and have an infancy:
there'd be first *remember*, then *remember that*...

and tiny clarities of stories would precipitate,

worlds hung quivering upside down in almost nothing
...and that *Once Upon A Time* was once,

yes, absolutely only *once*,

the only time there was.
But that's what I would not remember.

Heartland

For each turn off a main-er
      road onto a minor, each place
            less signed, more inside itself
(the turned back
      of a corrugated shed,
            its roof weighted with tyres,
three milk churns on their concrete shelf)

you could believe you're one step closer

to the heartland
      (as a loose black-and-white dog
            hurls out at your wheels) –
that the sheer lack
      of invitation is familiarity,
            as if the place could smell
belonging on you – one more blind bend,

it will shrug you in. Just one more skyline

and... The end.
      The edge. Unkempt
            unmitigated ocean,
its botherments, its wind-
      chapped patches and spats,
            its long insistence
on telling us something it can't quite recall,

dissolved in the thin rain that's starting.

Born here, all I know
      I remember is this:
            a dimming at the window,
wind-shudder, and afterwards
      drips. Drips from the low
            eaves. Slate on slate.
Beyond that, guesswork, and the weather

like a piece of elsewhere come to stay

as it did, bringing blow-ins,
        as it once brought wrecks,
                the drowned, the helped
to drown, the harvest
        of the storm; as it fell,
                leaching soil, pooling
in quarry pits, fell and then suddenly frothed

into steep streams, peat-brown, acid,

and back to the sea. Beyond
        heartland...heart-weather,
                leaching families
out of their thin farms
        to boats, to cities, to what
                the sound of wind
had schooled them for without their knowing:

elsewhere. Somewhere to make weather of their own.

for Mark Tredinnick, in north Cornwall

Storm Surge

It isn't the children
                    down here at the sea wall
          in the dim and storm-stretched
late dawn, the light
                    discomposed by the wind,

but the grey,
               the middle-aged and more-than,
          though the children we were, or
didn't dare to be, then,
                    are here with us too –

in that grin
               between neighbours who other days
          could pass for strangers, that glee
in our hop, skip and stumbling
                    back from the edge

when it breaks, a muck-
                    brown ruckus, wave-slosh
          going nowhere but suddenly
here, at large amongst us,
                    on the prom, a golem

still unsteady and out of its element
                    but, hey,
          it could like this life... then
crash-crumpling back,
                    so we're left, touched,

brushed against,
               a little breathless (the radio
     warned us; that's what brought us
running), half proud
                    of this wet sock, that slap

on the face,
                    the quite surprising weight of it,
            the great tidings it brings... still
with me now, hours on,
                            its mute melee and heft

in my closed eyes,
                    how a twenty-mile-wide swell
            comes unpicking the seam of itself
down the slant of the sea wall,
                            how it gathers up

its skirts and leans
                    into a head-down hunching run
            as if a mad Rococo ball turned
rugby scrimmage; one makes a break
                            down the touchline

to that final thud in the crook of the pier,
                            our *yes!*
            as if this was a kind of victory
for us too. To be
                    here. So very here. So very small.

Coming of Age

: when you start to hold pages at a distance,
almost out of arm's reach; likewise the detail
of days; when you start to see
the point of history;

when months go past the way weeks used to, seasons
a revolving door in which you seem to meet
yourself – again, *already?* – on the way
out coming in;

when the boom-box of a passing car leaves scorch-marks
on the air, smoke you'd choose not to breathe;
when you find yourself listening to quiet –
a-a-ah...! – like music;

when it grows on you, the urge to confide in the young
that secret they least want to hear: they too are
period already, pre-distressed like dodgy
antiques for posterity;

when you can't help it; when you *have*
to tell them:

then

A Briefer History of Time

First, there's un-time, Always
coming at you from unbidden angles.
Crying can control it,
slightly, or
you try a smile.

      One day
      the grown-ups close in to divide it
      for the first time, singing
      in a circle, with one candle,
      and a long knife, first slice of the cake.

For a time you will always
know when makes the what
makes the who you will be,
measured down to the half, the three quarters,
the eleven twelfths.

      Then that's childish. Wise up
      into years, though there's a subtle
      vowel shift somewhere between ten
      and teen. People notice that, and nod,
      but do not say.

Or say too much, and drink
about it. Something's coming, you
don't quite know what, as too-big-to-be-seen
as The Economy, or weather systems –
something called Of Age.

      The long haul
      is a kind of daylit night,
      sleep-walking, now and then a my-
      oclonic jolt off an imaginary kerb
      or precipice, a Decade...

And as for mid-life, or (paid off
imponderably, in instalments) middle age...?
How these *middles* square up,
actuarially? The more you have, well...
Do you even want it to compute?

      And now, mistier skylines, which are never
      skylines, or mist, when you get there.
      Views behind can be vastly
      small and deceptively clear. All I trust
      is what we measure between me and you.

When did we walk into the higher
mathematics, love? I haven't lost or chosen not
to keep count, just can't know
what fraction of what, back or forth, each year
might stand for. What one candle costs.

      Better to make each a single step
      together, each one naked long-
      stem rose. For you, here, (I'm
      not counting) one
      for now, for now, for

now...

Limited Edition

There, you caught it: the wind, that
                    something which is nothing
           but its moving and
the ways the world is swayed around it.

You cut its shape on the page. And
           water with its endless once-for-all
                    equivocations. And fire
in black and white, that least biddable

beast, which won't be called to hand
                    or heel. Once, we sat side
           by side and signed and signed
the limited edition, till we both, as one

man, burst out laughing: *I've forgotten
           how to! – I know, I'll do your
                    name, you do mine!*
There, never closer to the heart

of what made us both makers –
                    for a moment, almost no
           distinction between   us, the fire, the water

or the wind... which lifts now, Peter. On we go.

for Peter Reddick – 1924-2010

Mattins

And what if (this
        was the sore stiff body
                speaking; this was three a.m.)
                        it was all a mistake;

if it wasn't the cool
        and constant soul God loved
                but me?

(This was dark; this was the Mattins

                of the body,
          moving in its slippers
      through the cloisters of itself
to its offices.) Not

           me eternal, resurrected,
      made thirty again, nor
weighted down with gravegoods

but this – me as is, as am

in passing.
        If this rusty high C
            of sciatica, low
                  chime of heartburn

was the sympathetic quiver
        on my nerve strings
            of the choir

of angels? If *this* was theology:

imagine it. (This was the wince
        of the floorboard on the landing,
            the half-unwilling almost-
human timbre of the bathroom hinge.)

The body, shrugged clean

of the tricks and self-
                deceptions of the mind,
                        stepping out of (or into) itself
like the pool of Siloam,

in a dog-shake of spray-drips of light...

The body made new –
                not *young*... Not the body
                        in general but this one
in time, with its stuttering-out like stars

of brain cells, with what may be the hum

of a home in its ears, pipes clicking,
                an appliance shuddering to rest,
                        the bare skin chilling, and
each breath a little of its warmth

dispersed... Body washed in the blood

of its own veins, baptised
                from within with the kiss
                        and the commerce of oxygen,
of carbon, of their conversation. If it was *this*

God loved, if the secret got out...
                                        well, what then?

Fission

The sea-pool at Forty Foot:
a different deep
green like true ocean

and it's less a splash
than a quick Velcro rip
when our man meets the surface,

the mark on it instantly gone,

but he's put on a new skin
of bubbles (brighter for a moment
than he'd been in air)

or swaddlings, furling
tight and at the same time shedding
like a shuttle launcher at the gantry

with its umbilical cables dropping free

and I can see it, the trajectory,
the track the missile of him will pursue:
part of him's off and out into its element

while the other is whoopingly back
with a gasp, pump-and-paddling
the surface – *Jesus God*, he hoots,

that's bitter – to a ripple of applause

and he's hauling out onto the concrete,
stripped-pink-naked that he is,
no less of himself though I believe

I caught it then, the way they say
worlds split from any fissile moment, traced
in the Forty Foot collider, while him,

he's our man again, and welcome home.

I Am Those Clothes

left on the beach, folded fastidiously,
the name inside absconded.

They ran tests, but I told them nothing.
For a couple of weeks I was news.

People phoned in with their sightings
and confessions. False,

to a man, believe me.
In the end

I stood up, brushed sand from my creases
and walked, and went on walking

wondering who I could take it to,
this new and salty lightness at the core.

Pinches

A dirty shovel-shuck of it, damp
and hungry, turning snow
to chumbled slush
                   – your old
mate salt, old mucker
with a wink in the pre-dawn
lamplight and a snaggled grin,
who you wouldn't want leaving his prints
on your carpets, he
                    gets you out of a fix.

*

It was the tiny
            silver ladle
in its thimble-sized Aladdin's lamp
gave high tea
            at Aunt Sylvie's
(be it only corned beef mash)
                  such *taste*.

*

First Schoolbook German: *das
Buch... der Bleistift...* and
on page 3, *Die Salzmeister* –
Master Of the Salt Works – what?
so soon? as if we'd all have to meet him
one day and might as well know it from the start.

*

Only on the island of H.
is the winter so cold, the wind and waves
so grinding that the spray-fret makes salt snow.

*

33

He made it up, old Lot did. She was with him
through the years of exile, his racked shelves
of pickled grievance. She grew paler,
almost see-through. She'd not wanted to leave.
She never said, of course; she didn't need to.
He could taste it in her soup.

*

Dead Sea pastimes – well.
the only one, really: floating,
hands and feet in the air like grinning roadkill,
for the snaps. As if
it was mutual: this slippery-clingy salt soup
was repelled by you, would not quite have you,
as you were repelled by it.

*

It is said that he would dust the page with salt
before dipping his nib. Critics talked of his wit's
corrosions. Friends, of how his words would be preserved.
I think, when no one was looking, he couldn't resist
                         a quick lick.

*

              Oh, refined
to a glittering sharpness,
           the point of a pin
on a tastebud, Mistress
Salt will always have you
              wanting more.

*

That sort of morning: what comes out
of the oven is a brick – a hunk
of dead bread, reproachful. You forgot the salt.

Theses Written on Mud

1

That even starting from nowhere, going nowhere else, still simply
the numbering of things creates a sense of movement. An
illusion... as innocent as a painted backdrop hand-winched along
outside the window of a train in an early motion picture.

2

That I catch myself believing that's what they did – the hand-
winching, I mean – because I've written it, though I don't have a
flicker of evidence.

3

That this too is a kind of movie. Stop-motion animation of a
thought like Play-Doh or Plasticine.

4

That human figures made from Plasticine or Play-Doh, from
beach sand or mud, grow naturally between our fingers, where
they have a kind of life.

5

That somewhere a mullah might even now be denouncing a child
for doing that thing, unthinking, with blasphemous hands.

6

That God might, secretly, be eaten up with fondness, at the sight
of these blunt malformed child-made creatures. Sad too, knowing
that they cannot be allowed to live.

7

That somewhere in the floodplain mud, the alluvium, just outside
the city, where the shanties go up, is a lump that desires to be
golem.

8

That it was people's crying out for order, in unformed mud-voices, that set the golem's mud-tread going in the alleys of Prague.

9

That Golem, in his off hours, must have dreamed of river beds. Or been afraid to sleep, always hearing the drying and trickling away of his skin.

10

That the mullah too, like priests of many complexions, wants to get some order into the sticky, the palpable world. For its own good.

11

That, thus, a monk might nail a numbered list of theses to a door, thud, thud, and hear the echoes spreading, thus, thus, like the tread of boots.

12

That form, its formation, is in God's eye always reformation. Creation should be recreation, if that's so.

13

That the rabbi of Prague too watched his hands at their work, his hands turning to clay as he handled it, and wondered which was moulding which, what doing, being done.

14

That a word breathed in to it made all the difference.

15

That in the breath of 'thesis', melting one way into 'this is' and the other into 'these', we already have a hint of number.

16

That verse was born from voice-mud, in the hands of recreation,
with a hint of number, with a hint of tread.

17

That Thesis and Antithesis were a marriage made in Heaven, or
in Hegel. Ask their only child, Syn.

18

That there's always some danger when mud-shapes begin to
conceive of themselves. (Aside from God: Don't I just know!)

19

That each poor bare forked and early Play-Doh figure is
somebody's niece or nephew or great-grandchild's thought nearly
imagining itself, or who its maker is.

20

That to give a child a doll too lifelike, too eyelash-blinking-
perfect, is uncanny. Too made already. Too far from the true cloth
or true plastic, let alone true mud.

21

That now CGI can seamlessly make seem such perfect monsters,
we maybe have to hand-winch the backdrop, as clunky as this – to
get mucky, get mudded-up, clumsy as toddlers, just to reassert a
sense of what is (that something is) true.

Epstein's Adam

reminds you, if you've ever dug, how clay
comes up slabby and back-dragging, chunk
by spade-slick chunk. One flood away
from mud, from ooze, he's raised, half hunk,

half muscle-bound baby; he grapples the weight
of himself, still amazed where it came from, the will,
from nowhere. First the quick snatch, now the straight
lift... He's staggering, quivering, not to spill

what he's carrying: upturned, the flat plate
of his face, that holds nothing, that so wants
the sky – that *wants*... while the great
unwound-yet mechanism of him flaunts
itself, cock, pouch, a dull weight swung
by gravity, the trap as yet unsprung.

Jacob Epstein: Adam *(1938)*

38

In the Small Town

... of Peace, there's a splintering
          cat-fight. It's Saturday night.
Magda, Kirsty, again. The lads, knee deep already
     in lager and shots, wade in deeper,
          and there's talk of bottlings
and big bastard uncles, and I'll have you,
     pikey, cunt, you wait, and now

          the morning after. Peace
has this bruised light and a headache in it.
     It will have to heal
          and be swept, that spilled
self-pity, the splinters that will prick and bleed
     under each other's skin for weeks.

          And this is peace, yes, this
is not an aberration. If the shuttered arcade
     can't be rattled and still wake,
          still peace, just – if only
our hushed selves will do, then it was never

     Peace. Small town or seething
          banlieu, in the war zone even,
peace makes its incursions. The shared fag before.
     Or in the shattered stairwell,

          three kid soldiers holding her,
clothes ripped, at gunpoint; one waves her away.
     She's like his sister's friend, her

          with the buck teeth, Magda,
was it, and the stupid laugh, but you know, he knows,

     she doesn't deserve this, in the end.

The Rag Well, Madron

A close day. In-
        wardness. The sullen

humours of the place, its half-
familiar secrets. Its
              humidity.

We've picked our way
        through marsh scrub,

low goat willows.
standing pools of mud
           and hawthorns,

one suddenly
        in blossom:

multi-faded tatters
like a rainbow
           wrecked.

The rag well...
        Up close, each

is a torn strip
trim, tassel or skirt hem.
           Leave part

of yourself –
        a scar should show,

a rip, a patch,
a good blouse spoiled.
           It should cost.

Nor is this meant
            – it's not its humour

– to be beautiful.
Swamp blossom: an explosion
                in a laundry,

washouts from a warehouse fire,
            pure waste…

What we will give
to grief. What we'll pay
                for desire.

The Players

Somewhere in a square in the old world, by the Hotel Princip,
    by the Palace of Justice, somewhere in a park
        of clean gravel and poodle-cut trees

beside cobblestones seamed with tramlines, somewhere near
    a kiosk café whose waiter, in stubble and butcher-
        striped apron will fail to appear,

sometimes for days, at three wrought iron tables, bearing
    coffees concentrated to a fierce point, a black
        hole – one sip will suck you in,

turned to sparkling stone... Somewhere like this they sit, two
    old men, each one older than the other.
        Bending forward, they sit at a pace

from which the three-lane traffic is a shimmery smear,
    a mirage, oil on water, and the pieces
        themselves seem a fidget,

a jitter of cause and effect which leaves no choice but,
    now and then, to lift a hand... a moment's
        late appraisal, as the world

turns one more orbit. One
                moves. Looks up. The other
    nods. I've seen them at the black and white
        marble table with the raised squares

in the Garden for the Blind, a table like a plinth
    on which they are building ice sculptures
        of certain uncertainties, and

it is beautiful, very, they might say. If ever they spoke.
    (Kibbitzers do the chatter for them.) They
        live, if indeed they do,

in twenty worlds at once, all intercutting: *if, and if*
    not, then, and if then, not... Every
        thirty years or so, a bang:

slammed door or backfire of exhaust, and now and then
    a handgun. All the combinations shatter
        into flight, up

over rooftops, dewlapped gables, weather vanes
    to reform, circle, circle, homing
        on wherever we may be.

Ways to Play

Simultaneously. Blindfold. As an exhibition.
Lightning. Quick death. In bed, by candlelight,

with you, naked. In the original Persian.
For hours, for weeks, on a mind-blanking cruise.

In a tent, in the rain, in the mud. In a cream-
coloured caravan, with kids, in desperation.

On a red and white plastic travel set, tiny,
queasy, in the back seat of the car. To please

mum and dad, though not equally. Not –
that would be unlikely – to impress the girls.

Online, against names who might be any
body, age or sex. Against a deep machine.

For a place in the ratings. Face to face
with yourself, and solo, with the board

against a mirror. With human sized pieces
played by loudhailer from a first floor balcony.

To absent yourself from bruising playground games.
In a trench, in a foxhole, on the night before.

In reverse, to lose, where losing's winning.
With grave diplomacy, in place of war.

To take on an aura, like a psychiatrist's
accent. Or a Viennese beard. Because sense might be made

within sixty-four squares. Professionally.
With ruthless insouciance. Yes, to win, or to win

a reprieve. Because what smarter way is there
to lose? For escape. For the side. For your soul.

Hordes

A dozen raised cherry-pickers
in a lit yard at dusk, in a circle:
you might say, a *concentration*,
     a *conclave*, an *acclaim*...

whereas this dump of dayglo
bollards and cones, like an off-
handed cast of I Ching: a *mishmash*,
     an *abandonment*, a *disdain*.

What's the plural of many, when what
we make turns to itself, without us,
come into its own? Not hoards now
     but hordes of the things.

By Portway Docks we pass a fair field full
of auto-opportunities, *sans* number plates,
all blandish, brand and gleam
     and less identity

than the emperor's porcelain army,
each of which possessed at least
(was possessed by) a face.
     Your face, it could be,

in the windscreen, yours and mine.
Our names on a green surtitle. Drive
carefully. Abundance glimpsed
     in passing like a mile-

long TV showroom window flickering
in slightly differing widths and tones
and definitions. So our things
     become us, we

them. Do what they do. Smile.

Coprolite

As close as we're likely to get
        to stopping time
or possessing a world in the palm of a hand:

this not-quite-a-rock
        or thunder stone,
the Venus of Willendorf's kid sister.

A stomach-pump autopsy,
        core sample
drilled through a lifetime of suppers, each

with a flavour of *last*:
        the way it goes
when living in the suburbs of extinction.

Ask the permafrosted
        mammoth, ask
the Neanderthal tooth with all we need to know

about the daily grind
        inscribed on a back molar
sure as a microchip. You could start a new

religion with these,
        closer than a saint's ten
dozen finger bones. It would come down

to bread, or simpler:
        grain, leaves, rare
meat for a feast, and nowhere to go back to,

footfall, leaf-fall, snow-
        fall; age on age
pass through us, every time we sit to eat.

Waits

Sudden stagger-up voices
        – God, at this hour? – propped
against each other in rough harmony.
                It's not the local school,
no sign that they're a good cause
        or in any sense good news,
stumbling out of the unsilent night
             – is *that* the time
of year already? – an unholy din
        that kicks its clod boots
on your doorstep, thick with byre-
            muck and mud
from nowhere within centuries of here.

        They could injure themselves
on that rickety ladder of tune
        up to your window. Click:

the security light gets their uplifted
            faces (if
they're rosy-cheeked it's booze or bruise),
        palms out for, quick,
whatever small change you can rustle
          but too late:
they've woken the baby
        that no songs can lull,
no stories pacify... but cries
          and cries, poor
love, all through the night, through history.

A Pump in Africa

Here's water, as the human eye
can't see it. Maybe God's
eye, or a fly's,
            the mirror-ball
of timelessness, the almost-insubstantial
lacewing's gold eye, can.

Here's one tile of the broken
mosaic, one moment in free fall:
a loose shatter of water
in the wrestling of gravity
and surface tension,
              hangs

as chunky as windscreen glass
between the pipe's mouth (crudely
welded iron –
             in another life
it could have been a pipe-
bomb or a mortar) and

the boy's. The people running,
reaching for it, are a blur
and the story, where it ends,
if it's the first
             cough-gargle
of the pump, the first splash

on the skin, with a rust-eggy smell,
the first roll of the drops
in the dust
            or the last,
the photograph can't tell us,
and it all depends.

Towards a General Theory of String

- It starts with a stop. A point. A singularity, till... What if one day a full stop thought to face the other way, to be a full start – *ergo*, everything?

- And... bang. We try to grasp the point, but what if the point is that the point conceived of... somewhere else – and tried to be there, all at once?

- This figures on our flat-earth maps and minds as a circle. An ever-widening, astonished O...

- ... or an expanding empire. Outposts, farther frontiers whose real purpose is to stop us looking further. It usually fails.

- The original line, stretching its one-two-three dimensions (four) to lasso its own imagination. No wonder it snapped. Went haywire, like a ball of tangled string.

- You can try this at home. In any kitchen drawer or toolshed, string complicates itself. You don't need to suppose there is a God for this.

- Grandfather kept a jar called Bits Of String Too Short To Be Of Any Use. For God to be like this would be more to the point.

- How many random fibres make a fabric? Is it simply a matter of many, mess-multiplied, Mistresses Clotho, Lachesis and Atropos, or rolling around in their off-cuts till we come out clothed, by chance?

- First time in love, even a piece of frayed string round her finger, round his, can be the mythical, the quested-for gold ring.

- Taking a line for a walk: it goes rushing off into the undergrowth, on the track of its lost instincts. Or in widening tangents in the wide field, loosely anchored to our own dull plod.

- Drop me a line, he said, meaning a letter. Or maybe a lifeline in the unplumbed, immeasurable sea.

- Does every line have a nostalgia for the circle? *Ergo* dreams of Nirvana, full stop to the cycle of being, nowhere else to be, or need to be?

- On the other hand, and further than either hand outstretched – even a child's hands: *that* big! – what would it be to be an *endless* line, right round the earth, or curved space? Einstein. Or Columbus. Or a refugee.

- A plot line is a line that *Once upon a time...* Need I say more? Does it already have you on its string?

- Once we read tea leaves, the entrails of birds. Now we can smash a particle at the speed of light. In its unravelling threads we read the tale of the beginning.

- String Theory: we try to conceive of some connection, each particle a different length of tingling out of and back into nowhere – you, me, us, our different frequencies.

- What child will not pluck a taut string when she finds one? Trick some music from a huntsman's bow? Or, later, stroke it till it starts to sigh, then moan... then sing?

- And the stuff in the kitchen drawer? Be tender with it. It may just be playing Double Helix. Simply trying to find its way home...

- (*How long is a piece of string?* No answer but: *Cut,*

- *cut!*) ... like everything.

Senex

: a dry crackling word,

the sound of tinder catching –
the tribe round the flames, cold

slabs of night behind them;

the voice of the one by the fire,
becoming it:

that kind of old,

crisp, tetchy, liable to flare
– no time for smoulder,

and no truck with anything

but clarity. A little cracked?
No wonder: bones ready to snap,

not like the green-stick fractures of the young;

bones honeycombed, half air,
lightness that could blow away

(and will) but for the riffling glow

that holds the ash in shape, a page
handwritten, words still legible.

The young can't touch.

Beside this,
they feel insubstantial, and too much.

Fire Balloon Heart

Still too winter a night to be lingering but
off the track, beyond the shrubbery,

these two are struggling, in earnest,
tenderly, to get it up: their frail

near-globe of a papery fire balloon

lopsiding again and again
till they steady its saucer of pale

slack flame between them; wait,
lift it, help it, uncertainly, leave.

It's a red glowing heart. Aah,

you could say. Or: there are shopfuls
of Valentine kitsch. We're three

times their age, hearts as tough
as lorry tyres to have got us this far

though apt to trip and flutter – yours

with (the doctor looks up
from her stethoscope trance)

its murmur. Listen.
It says Steady now.

Take care.

The Shapes They Make

our two bodies, together...
and surprise us, waking

facing, in the knees-up,
chin-to-knuckle crouch

an archaeologist would recognise –

today, with hand to hand
raised, right to right,

half way between a high-five
and a handshake

like the glancing clasp of team-mates

or good rivals even, at the net,
the moment after,

the momentum still in their two bodies,
heel of hand on heel of hand, or

spent, past speaking and bent to their knees

like runners gulping air
or, emerging

on a narrow ledge at last,
at least, still roped together:

mountaineers...

Love in the Scanner

This is beyond touch: two young volunteers,
        shy now (he grins
    askance; the back of her hand
brushes his, their little fingers

link) among solicitious researchers,
        circumspection all round
    as they ease themselves in
to the bright human-cannonball tube

of the MRI, together. Snug
        as cavers in a sump.
    No velvet-draped four poster,
no box bed, was ever so private,

so exposed. The marriage contract sheet
        hung at the bridal
    chamber's window
with its wax-red seal was nothing to this.

Beyond shame, in a shuddering hum
        of magnets tracing
    what no I can spy,
however peeping... not even themselves –

inside – they're seen sliver by sliver,
        reconstructed on the screen
    in real time: soft maps,
continents colliding. Isthmus and estuary,

tides, shifting boundaries of flesh, barely
        distinct, embodied
    ghosts of fondness
and of matter's dedication to itself.

Call it *fuck* or *coitus*, say *make love*
                or the Biblical *know*,
       this is beyond it,
and it makes me want to touch

your hand as she his. We're as still
                as those two must be
     yet do what they came for,
here in the narrowing space

of our lives, with years and calm stars
                turning round us, reading
     us as we can't read ourselves.
So little space, so little *play* (and yet we do).

Epithalamium, with Squirrels

Saw this, today, and thought of you

two: there,
not there, the quantum flicker

of a squirrel, this-side-that-side
of the tree trunk,
rightside up or down,

an astonishment particle,
a pop-eyed quivering on claw-tips;

gone.
And I had to look sharp to be sure
if this was one

like a pun on itself performed
in mime, or... Yes, it was two

released in skitter-spirals, up,
down, helix, counter-helix: the play
of material things

in their nearliness, freak
mutations of the moment, weight-

less prestidigitations, always meeting
ourselves coming back
around the corner like the skyline

of a wild surmise.
And whether these new

sudden selves we are together are
the nouns, or whether
now we know that particles are spin,

vibration and momentum, it's the verb
of us that is the one true thing

is immaterial
beside this moment (everlasting
unto everlasting) that feels like return

to lightness, against all
the world's gravity. It slips between

words, as in *light... enlightenment... delight.*

for Liz and Bob

The Way It Arrives

... the moment, just by being there
already, once you notice – like a colour,
say, red, say, that shade barely a blush
short of vermilion,
                 that lifts
as a crisp wrapper lifts, out of everything
rush hour and gravity holds, on the gust
of a street draught or your sudden
readiness to see: red,
                 lipstick
(retro) now, now brake-light, now an ill-
judged geranium – just one millefeuille
flake of all possible wavelengths... The way
it takes us, as a solar wind
                 can drift
a supersensible contraption, square-rigged
star-junk with gold-plated microfibre vanes,
downstream and out into the always-
not-arriving, darkness,
                 twittering
its shreds of data home. The way we're
lifted, scattered, in sensations. Wear
a blink of red, love, and I'll find you
in the crowd, all through
                 the thinning
and departing universe, the distances
that sound like time, like colour, words
escaping sense: light
        year
              red
shift

Watermark

There's a line in the sea

made of nothing – as sure
as a watermark in paper

except shifting: just a stone's-
skip out, this straggling self-

negotiated boundary

like the isobar
between an accent and an accent,

different ways to articulate
light: grey dusk satin or matt.

If you doubt that it's real

ask the gulls: pert, light-touch
and tip-tilted black-headed gulls,

a trim mob of them, high-riding
as if not yet loaded to the plimsoll line.

strung along that seam

where the backwash of almost
the top of the tide stirs something up

from under – a fizzle of small food –
and spreads it like a deck of cards.

Snack-accurate, their beaks

pick at the fine froth. Speck
by speck. Then one, from one end, lifts

and the whole flock peels off into whirring
and whitening flight, a self-made wind,

        broadcast seed,

that regathers itself
a hundred metres down shore.

There they glow, still
trimmed wicks of attention,

        till the next flickering sweep

back to, approximately, where
they were. They stitch that line

while the light goes, work needful
as love. As hand on hand. We watch

        till we can barely see.

Small Songs of Carbon

Those oval nubs of rubbers
in (those days) every school-
boy's pencil case – sweets
sucked by the beast of carbon,
its black spit.

*

Up in the higher Hs
every pencil is a lethal weapon.
Sharpen it with care.
   Sloppy Bs,
on the other hand (mucky fingers)
just don't see the point;
   they are almost a fluid,
good for shading, moulded shapes,
not outlines, nearer, further... where
   we live, in tender blur.

*

Fire counts
in minutes – carbon,
    centuries.

*

The fine-as-grey-snow sift
from riddling the grate –
   one puff
and it stands in the air
beside you. Moves when you move.
   Won't lie down again.

*

The moment when the sweep's brush cocked
its implausible snook from the chimney –
like a secret, out,

what every family in the street
shared: soot.

*

Oh, and what can you say about diamond –
the same stuff as us, as life, but
gone to heaven, so
emptied of itself, all weakness, so
inhabited by light.

If you didn't love it, you would say it hurts.

Coming to Slow

Slow arrives, more suddenly
than quick can. Here is where Slow lives,

between shutter and click,
tick and tock. In no time. Say it's *relative*,

I see the old, the dim-doddery
one in the family the others don't get round

to visiting. But you do. Flinch
a little when Slow, now, takes you by the hand

and leads you outside, to the shock
of night air, to space and its clockwork, stars

that seem stopped in their tracks,
coils of glittering wire – the way a river wears

its bracelets, whips a steady
spinning top of eddy or exfoliates its never-

ending scales of light. Study
this, and what is quick, what slow, and where

are we? One moonless night
I tried to slow my pulse and breath to test

the speed of it, not the light
but the seeing, on the fifty-mile arm-stretch

of darkness that was Severn Sea.
Could I be still enough to count the flicker-blips,

their different frequencies, each me-
me sign among the masthead sparks of ships:

light-buoy, warning beacon, red,
white, green? Their telling pauses, a prickle of risk

on lethal waters, likewise a code
of comfort, silent morse whose slow-slow-quick

I couldn't hold, that human eyes
can't grasp: past, future in a present tense of flow

our language lacks. *Sub specie
aeternitatis...* We try. The first steps are slow.

for Wyn, at 50

A Walk Across a Field

A week of snow, slight melt, refreeze
and it comes to this: the ground
    withholds consent
    to every step;

it has us grappling, gasping, at each other,
    like the fond emergencies
    of young love.

Now my hi-tech walking pole
becomes a straw I clutch at,
    drowning nearly
    in the blank

expanse of frozen watermeadow,
    quivering with strain.
    This isn't a stroll;

it is a horizontal mountain, sheer
drops always at our feet,
    like any pavement
    for the very old.

No time or surface is quite level.
    Once-clear pools
    grow dim-eyed and tense;

they too thicken and bulge
to threatening opacities,
    who knows
    how brittle.

We make it back to the car;
    I count us in
    – me, you,

back from the ice age, to real time,
to the age we are. For now.
       One day, if I'm
       the one left

to remember longer, I'll remember this.

Several Shades of Ellipsis

1

... here, a shudder, in mid-sentence: a matter
    over which we'll draw a veil

– midway between the stage-magician's
    curtain and the frill

around the oh! the ankles of the Victorian
    table, you might think. No,

it's the niqab's *This far only am I here*
    for you. The watching.

Or the phone rings: all the time you take
    to reach it, then

a measured pause before the click, too
    long for comfort –

punctuation of its choosing, not yours –
    when you speak.

2

.... then again, there's the swoon
into the *petit mort* of punctuation: bliss,
    I could only assume

before we'd been there ourselves,
together. Still together, in small
    measure, for hours

afterwards, back in our separate
lives, but with our knowledge, silence
    down your inner thigh,
        its drip, drip, drip.

3

... then, the sentence that's backing
      away from the point
            (– point – point),
slipping out of the room leaving this,
      jotted, *Back in 5 min.*
          And no time. Or that
without even the words, so it might be a note
      from forever.
          Five minutes,
or less.   Yes, it might be that close.

4

... there, the jerky
hitch, then click-sway into place,
twitched by no hand, on its rail

of the crematorium
curtain, of which we'll say
no more, half grateful

to the clunky tact-machinery,
how it helps us to know
what we're willing to know

or not know – how to see
what we'd rather not see.

5

... way back, the spit
of hard drops on the window

is his father's black typewriter,
Olympia, and faulty even then,

a stickiness somewhere in among
its tensely nested levers, packed

like the gills of a toadstool; hesitancy
– hear it through the study door

or bedroom wall – unreadable,
not word but punctuation

of the night. The pause before
each hollow whack. Whack. Whack.

6

...or the stuttering out
of his words before the line's end: dots and scribbles were all

he had left of the text
of himself to refer to; how he'd begin in block capitals, urgent,

a ransom demand: one
letter, two; by the third it was wavering, then the decay

into scratches and blots – not
just the meaning but the one who meant it, stepping off

the marked path and into
abeyance. Mist. Our grey particles swirling. His old biro

stubbing till the paper
ripped. That's courage, then, to keep transcribing

stab, waver, tic: raw
data from a place that's neither here nor there, nor

in, behind, beyond.
Unbroken code. Him staring at it, frowning, as he once

did, taking pains to get
each petal and sepal and carpel of a single cyclamen,

drawing just what he saw.

7

...now, the snick
into flight at the lip of the ski-jump,
                    like a snapped sigh
its sharp edge, a wind that can turn on its heel:

now it's sky
for us, and it's nothing but tiptoe
                    on the fine line
of momentum, this flight that is also a falling,

as we must,
with nothing but a certain poise to hold
                    us true – these leaps
of implication we share, wobbling in clear

air, to crash
and crumple maybe but – tip-touch
                    my fingers as we slip
into the white space – love, not yet...

Blue Dot

About to slip back to bed, from the known-
by-heart dark, barely waking, from barely an edge between things,

me and things, you and me – there might be only one sleep

where we bob to the surface now and then
with the flotsam of separate dreams.

So far, the body's habit... but I've lingered for the chill

to give me back my surface, where I end, where I begin,
my faint blueprint on black. To feel the difference.

Any moment now – if, when – and I'll be distinct

beside you... like those mornings one of us
is up, dressed, cool and crisp-edged to the world, one

still in their skin, in that soluble state. To touch

then, or... not yet, like the moment just before
it strolled back, the Apollo Orbiter, came whistling

round the corner of the moon, from a sky quite without us

to earthrise. Where we live. In this chink
between fever and chill. The one possible zone.

Now you shift, and say my name. I'm home.

Hold tight, love, as we feel ourselves
diminish, to that blue

dot, caught in Voyager's last glance before

it powered down its camera. Stepped off the edge.
Became the rumours of itself. It won't look back again.

Brownian Motion

Not a draught or a shiver of footfall
        in the shut room, the Brownian
study – a book-cushioned hush,
        a bench brass-bolted to the floor,
the world as one held breath

        and yet it moves; a weightless
grain, pollen a century dead,
        on the gloss of the water that not
the least touch of the light moves,

        is hither-and-thithering. Blithe
indirection. He bends close
        as love. It's a step to the edge

of matter. If he closes his eyes
        the spark-specks on his retina

swarm. Nothing anywhere is still

        ...as now a ground of coffee
twitching on clear water in a white cup

        stops me: mute jitterbug alive
with knowledge in it, what we lost
        all those years since Lucretius:

that the clear space between thing
        and thing is all trouble... either that
or delight, *jouissance*, a fine
        discontent at molecular level.

Take this from the heart
        of things: that nothing will be fixed.
These are the angels on the pinhead.
        (Yes, stop, or believe you stop
and stare.) Little jazzers. They're having a ball.

72

Whereas

the slack shrug of the buddleia at the trackside, so at home on clinker,
  wears the burnt-out wicks of last year's mauve
    in a spirit of *OK for now*,
      not of *over*;
and whereas and notwithstanding that the legal mind, in its quest for,
  for once, the unassailable document, one with no chink
    into which a cavil could be inserted,
      thus, eschews
the poor comma, this, hardy weed of interstices, un-word that harbours
  meaning in its hesitation, one that could be hauled up
    in court and have nothing to say
      except *yeah*,
whatever and a glance at the window (where in early March already
  old Ma Buddleia's putting herself about,
    putting up her two-fingers
      of green);
and whereas and in consideration of the fact that so much happens
  in the slippage, between seasons, on ground
    no title deed can quite account for,
      as a crack in the brain
admits a colour or scent from way back, like a tune your parents'
  wireless seemed to sing, *oh lady of Lacuna*,
    in a language you didn't yet know
      you didn't understand;
and whereas all this is one moment, scribed as if in quill pen,
  in copperplate curls, like those eddies of air
    in which seeds are whirled up, in
      their season, in-
substantial as commas, by the slipstream of a passing train,
  still, I'll take to the stand, hand on book,
    hand on heart, to say Yes,
      I attest to this.

Translucence

        : with time
the skin thins; we become more see-through
as if the drip
        of it, passing, was diluting us.

      These summer nights
he can't sleep; his eyelids aren't enough;
he could long
        for the skin of the young,

      its heedless opacity,
how you could fold yourself inside it
deep.
       Live long, live longer

   and you'll see his eyes
still watching (what else can they do?)
through near-
        transparent lids

      at all hours, open now
to what nobody tells us: how we grow
into nakedness,
        no hiding place from light.

Thirteen Ways to Fold the Darkness

1

It was as if he'd gone to bed in mint white sheets, with pillows plumped the way his mother used to... *Night night, sleep tight. Mind the fleas don't bite. If they do, squeeze them tight...* None of your sloppy duvet lifestyle here, but crisp hospital corners. Each crease ironed to a razor's edge.

It was as if he'd gone to bed and dreamed of... sleep.

That sleep was like the sleep he'd fallen into, in a bed like the bed, in a room like the room, the night, the life – exactly like it, but its dark twin, in layers of grey-brown folded into black. Without depth, ironed flat.

Imagine that, to be without dimensions. You could layer us all in one bed, he thought – like shadows smoothed out onto shadows, every one there'd ever been. All comers welcome.

Think of the huge, the cosmic tidiness of that.

2

Once, in a four-year-old version of forever he'd lain making shadows on the wall, in the faint muddy street light through the curtains, just enough to make – *look*, with the fingers cocked just *so* – a bird ... a snake – *look*, slightly swaying – or two ears, a snout, mouth open: dog? Or wolf? He was never alone.

They lived, his shadows, in their fashion – they made friends, fell out, hunted, ate or otherwise consumed each other in strange grown up sorts of ways. They stretched out on the woodchip paper, growing taller, thinner. Flat. Look how they flowed and rippled round the curtain. It all seemed so much more... well, possible, with one dimension less. Yes, he could live like that.

It was a matter, at first, of lying very still. Of being your own shadow, folded in the shadows of your ironed sheets.

Can you iron a shadow?

Once, he saw her – washerwoman in the all-night laundry. She was silhouetted in a cloud of steam, her muscle-mountain shoulders, leaning away from him, into the sigh of the steam-iron.

Its huff and its spit. She straightened up, and if she turned now, with the iron hissing in her mitt, what then...?

Night night, sleep tight. Fold on fold, dark into light. Burnt umber, khaki, and black's the new white...

Night night.

3

Don't think he is naive about these matters.

We have our grown up fairytales as well. How – is it three, or four, or nine, or thirteen unimaginable dimensions fold into each other, universes ironed neat into each other's creases... He thinks Time is the little-'un, wriggling in between the other's knees and grunts and snores.

He thinks all this is true, just like the older fairy tales were. Not true in the sense of 'true', but... *true*.

4

In the flat house of sleep, the flat rain hangs in drops that can't fall, in flat gravity, off eaves of slightly greater darkness than the hardwood beams and panels, wood with memories so long that all they can do is tell their names over: ebony, bloodwood, ironwood, lignum vitae, nightwood, teak, mahogany.

5

Or think: Queen Victoria's mourning napkins... Because how could anyone abide the white of table linen? Or its absence. So...

With the same attention to detail, to the stiff starched crease, the small dark arts of folding, so...

What rides on the black lake of the table cloth, beside the silver gravy boat reflecting and distorting the little gas flames, scarcely blue; what glides without moving, by its single soup tureen, untouched and cooling:

one black napkin swan.

6

Always just at the edge of his hearing, the way the old folk said it, in the village tucked in the dark fold of two tors: *Her*, they'd say, and nod like high court judges. *She be gone to stay with Uncle Peat.*

A kind man, clearly, with a fair house, because none of them ever came back. It sounded like a home for waifs and strays. On bad days at home, he wondered if he'd sneak up there and see.

All this was after the carts stopped coming down the moorside, with their stacks of black turves, some still dripping; long after the old smoke-smouldered hearths had been bricked in, except in the Baskerville Arms, for the tourists.

Still, once every ten years or so, a child would disappear.

7

Peat colours: gradations of brown, shades of conker, cocoa, russet, umber, right through to sucked licorice... All deepening with time.

Peat textures: like the slowest baking cake, all husk and hair, the darkest rye bread, with that sour tang, smoky, pickled.

Peat-water: that flows out of the heart of the moor, out of dark clefts, finding a name for itself, like Okement, Tavy, Taw or Dart. One minute it's a froth like Guinness, then it's clear again, somehow at the same time dark and clear. Find a pool and dive in; you become a sepia print of yourself. Your nakedness, historical...

'tis clean darkness, his grandmother said. She swore by it. Launder your fine linen sheets in this, and peg them up between two thorns to dry, and you'll never have a poor night's sleep.

Or better still, cotton... bog cotton. You know those little white flames, on the high moor, flags of warning on a sudden too-green sward? When I was young, she said, my tread was light enough to harvest it, with time to get enough to spin and weave. Now I'm going to sleep, she said, sleep deep. And so she did.

8

Keeping house in a world of dark matter – yes, *that* side of things...

For every bedtime in this dimension, whether tuck-you-in-snug or end of the work-day, sickbed or deathbed or blinking-in-the-morning-after one night stand, not to mention the blotto ones, pits of no dreams, the skinny-dipping of the mind, there's one out there.

In each, there is your equal opposite, in its dark bedtime. You and other-you, tossing, untouching, at the same coordinate in space, itched, is it by dreams of each other? Until one day you thrash, the film between you rips like an old sheet, and you fall into each other's (which is to say, your own) embrace.

9

His maiden great-aunt Maisie, with a steam iron, she was a philosopher. Her smoothing out of every wrinkle, *there* – now fold, *there, there*. Every angle a right one. She could do it in the dark. Maybe she practised that way, like a ninja. *There...* If she was not so frightening, he'd have ditched his books and studied her; he'd have sat at her feet, as...

QED, she ironed out a perfect fold in logic, so the edge of a term meets the edge of a term, like a small mathematic universe in which every thing is what its definition makes it, this and nothing else, so in agreement you could say (she didn't; this was *not* her word or way) they kissed.

10

The hiss, the kiss of air brakes, suddenly from outside in the street. Or was it his own breathing, from outside his dream? Was it one of those moments, an *apnea*: the steam pump sticks, the leather bellows rests, shut like a dark moth's wings...

...then a click: the world releases, flows back in.

11

The earth irons us flat: a plane, a bedding plane... what's all this but an age-long lying down to sleep? Mud, darkening to mudstone, rusty ochres bleeding in... Now a carbon forest, in a swamp, relaxes; now a peat bog, wearied by its introspections, lies down deeper in itself. Oh, weary carbon, as the pressure of its sleep turns it to coal.

The hiss of steam, clouds boiling off in weather. The mountain-muscles of her shoulders as she bends, in the night laundry. Oceans breathing in the sun.

The strata, fold on fold.

12

Or here's another way. (He recommends this, but can't master it)
Just not to say.

13

Night night. And dreadfully, but not unkindly, he is tucked in. There. Sleep tight.

Dark plumps the pillows. Dark sheets tucked in round the corners, tucked in under, crisp and tight. The wood mush of the ancient forest, sinking to its knees, goes to grey, goes to peat brown. Black. Sometimes it smoulders underground, all by itself. All that energy sleeping. Tucked in.

There.
Sleep tight now.
Can I have a story?
Hush.

It's only carbon dreaming. Try not to get frightened if, once in a million years or so, you dream that you wake.